FEAST

Poetry By
Maureen McDole

All poetry contained in this work is the original work of the author.

Published by St. Petersburg Press
St. Petersburg, FL
www.stpetersburgpress.com

Copyright ©2021

All rights reserved. No part of this publication may be reproduced, distributed, or transmitted in any form or by any means, including photocopying, recording or other electronic or mechanical methods, without the prior written permission of the publisher, except in the case of brief quotations embodied in critical reviews and certain other noncommercial uses permitted by copyright law. For permission requests contact St. Petersburg Press at www.stpetersburgpress.com.

Design and composition by St. Petersburg Press
Cover design by St. Petersburg Press and Lily James McDole,
Artwork by Lily James McDole

Print ISBN: 978-1-940300-41-2
eBook ISBN: 978-1-940300-42-9

First Edition

Books by Maureen McDole

Exploring My Options
Longing For The Deep End

For Lily James

"She must find a boat and sail in it. No guarantee of shore. Only a conviction that what she wanted could exist, if she dared to find it," -Jeanette Winterson

"We are living in a storm where a hundred contradictory elements collide; debris from the past, scraps of the present, seeds of the future, swirling, combining, separating under the imperious wind of destiny." - Adolphe Retté

Contents

Feast · 13

All That Is Required · 14

The Fine Art
of Postponement · 15

Control Freak · 17

I Am The Wind · 18

Her · 20

Pen to Paper · 22

The Hens · 23

Lightning Fast · 24

The Suffering Bind · 26

Uncontrollable · 27

Reflection · 28

Rocks In My Pockets · 29

Discovering My Personal
Defects · 30

Playing With Dolls · 33

Dear One · 34

The Tooth Fairy · 36

Chicken · 37

Love Out Loud · 38

A Boyd Hill Kinda Day · 39

The Reminder · 40

Jersey Daydreams · 42

Selfish · 44

Bug Life · 45

Foreclosure · 46

High · 47

Solar System · 48

Fine Wine · 49

Envelope · 50

The End · 52

Jellyfish · 53

Breaking Up · 54

Color Theory · 55

Knocked Down · 56

Moving On · 57

The Choice · 58

Can You · 59

The Big Bang · 60

The Romantic · 61

Deep Love · 62

Down the Rabbit Hole · 63

The Lover · 64

Love Me Perfectly · 65

Superpower · 66

Love's Alchemy · 67

Fear Quilt · 69

The Thief · 70

Untitled · 71

Bullshit · 72

Disconnected · 73

Going to the Bookstore · 74

Irises · 76

Be the Change · 78

More Rope · 79

Seesaw · 80

Modern Life · 81

Present Moment · 82

Sword · 83

The Passing of the Old Guard · 84

About the Author · 85

Feast

I am hungry

I am not defined by my desires
I will not be silenced for my thirst

I do not doubt my talents
I feast on them

The meat of mediocrity does not feed me
There is no shame big enough to devour me

I am hungry

I crave construction
I am built to thrive

The deliciousness of life is mine

All That Is Required

When I was younger, I liked to label things,
put everything in little boxes
that I could store on my mind's shelf.

I felt in control that way,
everything nice and tidy.

Yet, life does not work that way.

People do not like to be labeled.
Love is too big to be contained.
Nice and tidy gets boring.

What do I do with this information?
How do I feel safe in a chaotic world?
People die, friendships change,
and the words do not always come.

Trying to find an answer
to something that is unanswerable
was part of my original problem
and blind faith,

that that I will be safe,
is all that is required.

The Fine Art of Postponement

I am bored with the fine art of postponement.
This is it. This is my life.

It's time to stop waiting
for some distant day or night.

Where everything is perfect.
Where everything is right.

When there is only peace
and no fight.

Even without wind,
a kite is still a kite.

Control Freak

I don't know how to relax.

If I stop moving
the earth will spin
off its axis.

As if I am that powerful!

Being damaged
creates this contradiction,
this crux in my mind.

I feel so powerless,
as if I stopped constantly creating
my reality; pushing my
life forward

I know in my core

that the moon
would fall from the sky.

I Am The Wind

I am the wind
I am the wind
I am the wind

If I say it enough times
It will be true
Only I can harness my power
I will not be held by you

I can blow your house down
Or cool your cheek
I have the strength to erode
Those who mistake me for weak

I will rise above naysayers and detractors
Float above their heads
Be light enough to carry a feather
And fast enough to break ahead

It can be a lonely life
Being the wind
I touch everything
But have no kin

I can generate electricity
Carve away stone
Yet most of my life
Is spent exploring alone

I dry rain on the sand
I make the trees dance
I can blow away bodies

With one little glance

I am the wind
I am the wind
I am the wind

If I say it enough times
I will get over my doubt
And finally begin

Her

I want to know her,
my gentler half;
hear the secrets
she whispers.

Yet, I wrestle her.
She can't be trusted.
My fragile shell-translucent-
in my desire for her love.

She sees right through me.

We are all walking around wounded,
screaming for relief,
looking in the wrong places
for healing.

We somehow think it's not enough
being enough.
So, we give
until we break.

The fissures in our facades
want to grow flowers,
want the light
to shine through.

She smiles at me,
my stronger half.
I feel taunted.
I feel tangled.

She doesn't notice.
She is too busy dancing.

Her attention is elsewhere.
She has no time for my neurosis.
She plants new roses.

She is following the sun.

I drop in a huff
and with a puff,
she dismisses my drudgery,
caught up in the luxury of being alive.

I say, *What's wrong with me?*

She says, *Nothing.*
You are all lovely, all light.

Don't worry, she says,
everything is alright.

Pen to Paper

Most people can't do what I do.
They love to suggest real jobs for me.
They believe that the writing life
is unsustainable.

I want to reach out and hug them
for trying to help but,
they misunderstand me.

My currency is ink on my hands.
Blank pages are bank notes.
The only security for me is pen to paper.

The Hens

The practical hens
cluck cluck cluck.

They say I should change my life.
Look at your luck.

It ran away from home.

I long to scream,
We don't feed on the same food!

Nine to five
will be my tomb.

Their God is money.
I follow the moon.

Lightning Fast

What does one do
when they come to the end
of all they know?

A mixture of anxiety
and anticipation
courses through my veins.

I know I will never be the same.

I am floating between my future and past,
the present never lasts.

Things change
lightning fast.

I might as well have a blast.

The Suffering Bind

For the first time in my life
my past, present, and future

are swimming together.

No arguments about who did what.
No debts to be scored.
No sense of entitlement
or obligations to fulfill.

No drama to escape.
No feelings of guilt.

No one has power over me.

No grudges weighing me down.
No need to explain
or process or assimilate.

No weight on my spirit.
My body.
My mind.

I have unwoven myself
from the illusion of time;

the suffering bind.

Uncontrollable

I am uncontrollable.

If you took away
my paper and pen

I would memorize
my poems in my head

which you couldn't touch
even if you shot me dead.

Reflection

All the reflections
of the outside world
are meaningless

if we don't like
what we see in the mirror.

Rocks In My Pockets

Why do I keep
letting others

put rocks
in my pockets,

when all I want to do
is float?

Discovering My Personal Defects

Half truths and self-denials
sputter within me; they try to take root.

I know I am golden, deep down,
but my self-love radar is on the fritz.

After years of static behavior
and false starts

the clouds whisper *worthlessness*;
my atmosphere is charged with crisis.

I am bored to death
with my story.

Days wasted in bed.
Praying to be rescued, redeemed, renewed.

Silence.
No response.

This proves I am right;
I am utterly completely totally alone.

After years of this
I decide to peep my head into life, look around.

I am bored
with being a victim.

I see so many moving parts.

We are all interconnected.

I see similarities in stories;
we are all in a cosmic dance towards wholeness.

Each wanting to let go of the wheel
and find our true lane.

Our intertwining creates
a chaotic simplicity; synchronicity.

That keeps on calling
us home.

And this realization
keeps me from feeling alone.

Playing With Dolls

We are drowning in doll limbs
and broken bits
of unrecognizable toys.

Our five year old hums,
as she rips apart
her clothes drawer
to find the perfect outfit.

She has no concept
of good clothes and play clothes~
everything is play to her
and definitely good.

Somedays I feel
so far away from these concepts.
I forget to find joy in play.
I feel every other word,
but good.

I pick up a plastic leg and an arm.

The disembodied doll's hair is astray.
I often feel this way.

I then realize I need to play,
until I can put myself together again.

Dear One
For Lily James

Dear One,
if I could give you everything I would,
but life is an infinite path of becoming.

The capillaries of our days teem with new life.

Their nutrients come from multiple sources:
some singed with heartbreak,
some tinged with remorse.

I do promise you, if you take the time,
there is magic everywhere you look:

under every rock,
in every crevice,
around every corner.

Dear One,
if I could give you everything I would.

I wish I could create a picture-perfect life for you;
your own Garden of Eden.

There you would have no worries,
never hurry,
and always feel loved.

But then you would miss out on so much.

You would lose lessons learned
that make you yearn for more,

for that creative desire
is what causes your Earth
to continue to spin,

and your life to rotate towards joy.

The Tooth Fairy

Your first tooth is loose.
You have waited months
for this~wiggling your teeth
to test their fortitude.

They say dreams of teeth
falling out mean change-
transformation.

Our house is intoxicated
by this thesis at the moment.

Six-year-old changes.
Career changes.
Mental health changes.
Relationship changes.

If only our worries
could be placed under pillows
and transformed
towards good, come morning.

Chicken

We were walking to our neighborhood bookstore
on a gorgeous Florida fall day,
the kind we wait all summer to witness.

Our daughter starts to jump
over the cracks in the sidewalk.

"Step on a crack, break a chicken's back!"
"Chicken?" I asked.

She shines back at me
and without skipping a beat,
she responds:

"I don't like saying Mother, so I changed it."

Love Out Loud

Her little hand grabbed his
in the parking lot of the grocery store.
62 years separated them.

She did it unconsciously.
He seemed shaken.

I told him, "Daddy, we like being affectionate."

He flinched a bit.
"Oh, it's fine. It doesn't bother me."

I smiled the biggest smile.
I never felt more proud.

I was breaking family curses,
by teaching my child
to love out loud.

A Boyd Hill Kinda Day

I try to keep up as my daughter
and her pack of friends
run ahead of me, their hair the color
of the sandy trails beneath our feet.

I am the elder in this scenario,
but the wilderness, their wildness
is contagious.

I throw off my adult disguise
and run free with them.

We are having a Boyd Hill kinda day.

The heartbeat of nature, its rhythm
has no comparison.
It allows us to strip down to our essence,
brings us back to what makes us alive.

My father used to bring us here when we were children.
He softened in nature,
and quickly shed his adult disguise
to run free with us.

I have returned here over and over
throughout my life,
in time of crisis and joy
to have a Boyd Hill kinda day.

Where I can feel ageless,
boundless and wild,
running free
on the sandy trails beneath my feet.

The Reminder

"You live a great life, Mom."
She says as she dresses the dog.

"Why do you think that?"

"You can have chocolate and lollipops
anytime you want and
you are a writer."

She is right. I do live a great life,
I just needed the reminder.

Jersey Daydreams

Riding the bus on the Jersey side
I nudge your seven-year-old self
to look across the Hudson
at the NYC skyline-

so many lives
bustling about,
dreams being made
and broken.

"That's nice," you say.

Don't you realize
how fortunate you are?
You get to go on
grand adventures,
exploring places different
from where you were born.

"I am hungry," you say.

Your young mind is
nestled safely; unencumbered.

My adult mind
regularly crashes,
while narrowly
escaping one
existential crisis
after another.

"I am thirsty," you say.

The basics.
The bone and marrow
of life.

Simplify.
Trim the fat.

You remind me daily
to live like that.

Selfish

My eight-year-old daughter
asked me today
what the word selfish means
after hearing it on TV.

I was astounded that
she made it eight years
without becoming
familiar with its connotations.

I felt proud no one
had called her that.
It's not a part
of her vocabulary.

I told her it's when you
only think about yourself,
but it's not always a bad thing,
especially if she needs to set aside
time for her art.

I told her women often
brush aside their time for others
and it isn't healthy.
Moderation is the key.

I told her sometimes,
I need to be selfish
to be me.

Bug Life

My daughter catches ladybugs and caterpillars,
housing them in a mason jar
to observe with her magnifying glass.

We help her put in leaves and grass,
so the space won't feel alien to them.

A new love relationship
is like that
you are taken out of your natural habitat
to observe each other up close.

You bring trinkets; parts of yourself
with the hope
of not getting lost completely.

After a period of time,
we tell her to release the bugs,
so they can go their own way.

Lovers must also do the same,
for we all have our own paths to discover,

and some love
is not meant to go on forever.

Foreclosure

The house we bought together
is crumbling; ivy and weeds
overgrowing the eaves.

The earth is taking it back.
The bank is taking it back.

We are taking our vows back.

The marriage we built together
is crumbling, addiction and indifference
overgrowing the eaves.

Neither one of us is willing
to fix what's broken,
to stitch up the bleed.

High

I can do nothing for you,
no matter how hard I try.

It's one of my lifelong questions,
why

do you feel the need
to constantly get high

and let life
pass you by?

Don't you see-

you have been
gifted with the sky

and if you listened,
revelations from on high.

Solar System

I will not crash
to the earth,
because of your brutality.

You try to tether me
with your insecurities

and shoot me
out of the sky
with your words.

Your blackhole
is not my problem.

I am my own solar system,
unaffected by your force field.

Fine Wine

What if things had been different?

What if you had been
the man I needed?

Our love overflowing,
flooding the fields we tilled together.

The grapes we grew
fermented; unencumbered.

Every night we celebrated,
toasting our success

of not becoming a statistic.

What if we stayed together,
aging like fine wine?

Envelope

I want so badly to tell you how I feel,
but it will make no difference.

So I stuff the love letter
into the envelope of my heart

and leave it there,
undelivered.

The End

I finally knew it was over
once and for all

that it was time
to stop grasping

when all you had
to offer me

were bruised
broken memories.

Jellyfish

When a marriage ends, you have to extract
yourself from all the ways you have grown together.

Two jellyfish, intertwined.

Your tentacles are woven together
making a home, a means of travel,

a place of protection;
nourishment.

Strand by strand you must loosen,
sometimes quickly, by force

or it's done the most painful way,
inch by inch,

because you both still desire the other,

but you know you can no longer
swim together.

Breaking Up

Embryonic tears
full of dreams

unfertilized.

Color Theory

I am in pieces.
Ripped apart, grieving.

A dream died.
A marriage.

Somehow, some way,
I have to rebuild
my entire worldview.

I have to find a way
to see life again,
in a bright hue.

Knocked Down

Multiple blows
to my heart
When the dust settles
I am torn apart

I feel too barren
to start over
to begin anew

but I must remember

the soil was tilled
before the flowers grew

Moving On

The ghosts of my past
ring in my ear.

People I have broke bread with-
know all my secrets.

My heart, promised to them-
forever.

They are shadows now;
dust storms,

on what was once a fertile plain.

The Choice

If I was to sit down
and tell you all I have been through,

perhaps your jaw would drop,
or you would tell me to stop.

Suffering is all relative,
each experience personal
and unique.

Everyone deserves a chance to speak.
Everyone deserves to have a voice.

But, after all the talking
and discussion is done,

healing and forgiveness
is a choice.

Can You

How do you trust again
when you have been betrayed?

People change.
They do.

The question is,
can you?

The Big Bang

New life.
New adventures.

New friends.
New home.

My previous life imploded.
I feel so alone.

To get the lay of the land,
I'll have to throw away
my old plans.

My life is consumed
with looking everywhere
for a helping hand

and solid ground
on which to stand.

The Romantic

She fell in love
with books and stars
and boys with far away
looks in their eyes.

They sent arrows
through her heart
their intentions miles apart
from what she deserved.

She lived on fire
and she loved,
guided from above,
trusting the dove of peace.

She knew one day
she would get her wish,
her trueist wish,
her one true kiss.

Deep Love

Do you know what it's like
to have someone
reach so deep into you

that they touch your other side?
Stretching you open wide.

Leaving you
with nowhere
left to hide.

Down the Rabbit Hole

The first time she saw him,
his smile was a doorway;
she doubted it immediately.

She felt that was the safe approach,
based on years of hurt.
She knew they would never work.

She was familiar with closed doors,
with closed signs; no love behind.
He saw within her bewildered stare,
a vulnerable girl in there.

His doorway was open wide.
It beckoned her inside.
Her darkness gravitated to his light,
maybe things would be all right?

Down the Rabbit Hole they fell:
two strangers, in its spell.

She kept expecting the abuse to come.
She kept expecting his interest to wane.
She kept expecting the drama, the pain.

It never came.

Slowly she healed and
"I love you" was exchanged.
At the bottom of the Rabbit Hole
they both were changed.

Her weeping wall came crashing down.
Through his doorway, love was found.

The Lover

In you walk and my instinct is to loathe
For all the roads in which I do adore
I was quickly burned; hand to a stove
I knew, love was a curse I would abhor

You grabbed my heart and filled it plenty
Quietly all my doubts felt useless and moot
After the kisses came in amounts of twenty
I felt a goddess and in your eyes a beaut

Into my thoughts you began to creep and haunt
My tears did dry, in rushed belief
All my years of sorrow and want
Were washed away, in rushed relief

I relaxed and settled within your cove
Into love's embrace, I ran and dove

Love Me Perfectly

The way you love me
fits me perfectly

Squeezes into
my dark places

that I didn't know I had

Warms up
all my cold spots

Ties up my
loose ends

The way you love me
fits me perfectly

This free spirit
doesn't feel caged

My vulnerabilities are soothed
All my rage is contained

Superpower

There is a point in a relationship
when you know the next step
takes you towards possible heartbreak.

You so desperately
want to save yourself the hurt
and run in the opposite direction,

towards safety, but the warmth
of their touch and their breath
on your cheek has bewitched you

and you realize that your vulnerability,
to risk everything for love,
is a superpower

and you are tired
of playing it safe.

Love's Alchemy

If there was a way to gauge Love,
we would all carry around rulers and scales,
measuring and weighing,

until we got our fair share
and then we would feel satisfied
and our hearts, full.

But, Love is not a liquid,
a gas, or a solid.
It cannot be contained;
it changes shape- rearranges.

Some lovers know this.

They know instinctively
they must remain
unattached to the outcome
their tinkering produces.

They delight in the mystery,
so they keep mixing and testing,
until they find what works for them.

Because the best kind of Love,
keeps dancing like the spheres do,
even though it knows,

the Universe is constantly contracting
and expanding its shape all around it.

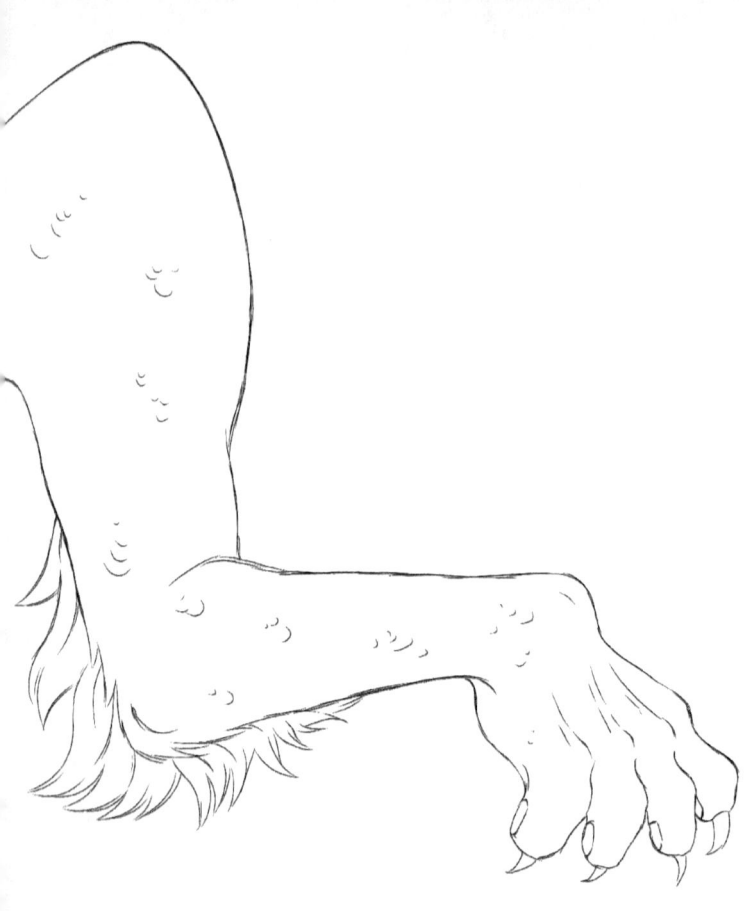

Fear Quilt

Scraps of fear,
a patchwork quilt
of grievances

that we try to wrap
around ourselves
to keep warm

but the cold still
creeps in

for we are full of holes.

The Thief

I was living the American Dream
and it turned on me.

My car wanted to eat me.
My house wanted to devour my soul.
My lawn choked my neck.

The electric bill left a hole
where the money to travel would be.

So I left it all behind
and took back all it stole.

Untitled

We are all trying
to find our own way,
our one true lane.

"You can choose
your own adventure!"

That's what they want
us to believe.

But, then they draw
the roadmaps
and offer incentives,

if you take their route.

Bullshit

Eat shit.
Buy shit.
Take shit.
You are shit.

Society encourages this bullshit.

Disconnected

We followed the rules.

Mom is frazzled.
Dad is absent.

The internet and strangers
are raising our kids.

We thought we would be rewarded.
We thought everyone would be healthy,
happy, and thrive.

We have the money to show for it,
but no one feels alive.

Going to the Bookstore

I am going to the bookstore
to look for redemption
I cannot find outside.

Outside is a reflection;
manipulations and lies
to forward the machine.

"Do things our way;
forget your dreams."

They pile on the bullshit;
it gets deeper and deeper outside.

Burrowing in a stack of books
is the only place to hide.

Irises
Inspired by Alex Katz's *Flags*

1.
This poem was supposed to say everything.
It would be the balm to heal all our hurt.
It would seal the divide in our country
and stitch together our grievances.
Poetry is that powerful.
Do you believe me?
You know you want to; you do.

2.
We are all walking around wounded.
Some people's wounds are louder and brighter than others.
They are flags attempting to claim their sovereignty,
but sometimes they only announce their hate.
I want to ask those who wave flags of intolerance:
Why are you letting the monster grow within you?
Don't you know if you feed it, you give it life?
You then become the monster.
The monster is not outside you.
It is you.

3.
Let me be clear, there isn't one right way to live, but
the Iris whispers: Faith; Wisdom; Hope; and Valor are
good places to start.

4.
You fear getting comfortable; there is a guilt that wasn't there before.
You know you must do somethIng.
You love your country.
You now feel like a refugee.
The scenery has changed.
Your country is living a story that you wouldn't write, let alone read.
The great God of Fate has said "Set Change!"
Everyone now needs new costumes,
when you were just getting comfortable in your own.

5.
The Iris was named after the ancient Greek Goddess Iris. Her rainbow robes were said to connect Heaven to Earth. If only she could come to us now, and transform our frustration and fear into the colors of love.

6.
There are many people more vulnerable than you. You know this.
You are not special.
But, you are kind.
You are a good parent.
You give back to the community in every way you know how.
This has to be enough.
This poem has to be enough, because it's the best that I could do for you, right now.

Be the Change

To save the world
You must save yourself

Find joy in delight

It will spread like a wave
and inspire all those enslaved

More Rope

The dominant narrative is:
Life is not a fairytale.

There are dragons and wars and darkness.

I believe in happy endings.

Redemption in kisses.
Triumph of good over evil.
Light at the end of the tunnel.

What happened
to make people so jaded
that they give up hope?

Don't they see,
that there is always
a little more rope?

Seesaw

Life is like playing
seesaw with yourself

Try to find the sweet spot,
the perfect balance

Not too hard
Not too soft

Up and down you go

Not too fast
Not too slow

Modern Life

Modern life is a corn-fed cornucopia
of theories to question

Some have merit
others threaten

Some heal
others are distressing

The main point
is to focus on the blessing

and trust the life lesson

Present Moment

Most of our thinking
is either in the past
or the future

Focus on now
then you won

The prize is the big picture

Sword

Once I set down the shovel
that for most of my life
kept me from being
buried alive

I could pick up the sword
that was waiting
for my inner warrior
the whole time

The Passing of the Old Guard

Fear-based living is boring.
The Old Man is snoring.

He is snug in his bed,
with nightmares in his head,

while we dance and celebrate a new morning.

About the Author

Maureen McDole was born in St. Petersburg, Florida. She is a direct descendant of carnies, carpenters and fishermen. Her first book of poems, *Exploring My Options* came out in 2006. Her second poetry book, *Longing for the Deep End* was released in December 2011. She has a BA in English Literature from USF-St. Petersburg and a certificate in Arts & Culture Strategy from University of Pennsylvania. Her poetry has been set in a variety of different ways including: film, dance, spoken word, art installations, Sprechstimme, and traditional vocal works. She founded the literary arts organization, Keep St. Pete Lit, because she believes wholeheartedly in the power of literature to change the world.

"Feast is a book about transformation, redemption, loss, and hope regained. It's a poetic journey of rebellion, love, art, motherhood, marriage and divorce; all the joys and sorrows that make life worth living."